Bibliographic information published by the German National Library:

The German National Library lists this publication in the National Bibliography; detailed bibliographic data are available on the Internet at http://dnb.dnb.de .

Imprint:

Copyright © 2007 GRIN Verlag, Open Publishing GmbH
Print and binding: Books on Demand GmbH, Norderstedt Germany
ISBN: 978-3-656-86435-6

This book at GRIN:

http://www.grin.com/en/e-book/284775/history-and-characteristics-of-us-sitcoms

Irina Wamsler

History and characteristics of US-sitcoms

GRIN Publishing

GRIN - Your knowledge has value

Since its foundation in 1998, GRIN has specialized in publishing academic texts by students, college teachers and other academics as e-book and printed book. The website www.grin.com is an ideal platform for presenting term papers, final papers, scientific essays, dissertations and specialist books.

Visit us on the internet:

http://www.grin.com/

http://www.facebook.com/grincom

http://www.twitter.com/grin_com

History and characteristics of US-sitcoms

Irina Wamsler

Inhaltsverzeichnis

Introduction... 3

1.   The history of sitcoms.. 3

2.   Characteristics of sitcoms 4

   2.1.   Strands and stacks.. 7

   2.2.   Canned laughter.. 7

3.   References (including additional literature)... 9

Introduction

The scripts of comedies imitate real life and fulfill the audience's needs in everyday lives. That means people like to relax while watching other people's daily lives including love, friendship, or working life. They want to escape from the pressure they had during their own day and enjoy funny and easy-to-understand-shows. Additionally, humor gives, as Bärmann (1989) claims, the audience a chance to breathe.

The evolution of TV series from the beginning of this genre of TV shows in the 1950s until today is important. The first TV series were comedies and variety shows but soon this concept was replaced by sitcoms. During the 1970s and the 1990s sitcoms changed as well as society. Rapidly, new issues like friends, emancipation, or the role of the family has changed. "The correspondence between reality and fiction has become in fact the most important thing for the public: present TV series want people to recognize themselves in the fictive and unreal characters." (http://www.periwork.com).

In sitcoms or television shows, humor arises in communicative situations, where situational humor erupts spontaneously and where laughter is the desired and calculated effect, prepared by scriptwriters. In the last decades two different forms of so called 'mass humor' have grown a lot in the United States, as Marc (1989) claims. He differentiates between situation comedy and stand-up comedy. Stand-up comedians represent their feelings and ideas in a funny way, whereas the sitcom "is the technology of the assembly-line brought to art" (Marc 1989: 13). In contrast to stand-up comedians, actors in a sitcom mainly have no contact to a live audience..

1. The history of sitcoms

"The so-called golden age of American humor" was in the 1920s and early 1930s (Goldstein 1999: 244). Gender based humor, class conflict, and the modern world were the major topics of jokes. This genre of comedy, which originated in the United States, was actually developed for the radio in 1922 (Mack 2002: 6). *Amos 'n' Amy* pioneered in 1930 (Bärmann 1993). In the 1950s, family sitcoms became very popular and in the 1960s this format was adapted to television. *I love Lucy* (1951) is the forerunner of all sitcoms dealing with the problems of emancipation a woman has. Mainly, the family or the working life is in the center of interest. *Bachelor Father* (1957) illustrates the life of a single-parent who raises his children and went on dates at the same time (Marc 1989: 78). In 1961, the *Dick Van Dyke Show* was the first sitcom which entered the "world of work" (Bärmann 1993: 14). *The Brady Bunch (1969)* showed the life of a patchwork family. Harmony is the key word for sitcoms in the 1960s. Due to the Vietnam War and the civil rights, Americans "found refuge in visions of Americas premetropolitan past and fantasies of witches, genies, and nannies who could do the vacuuming by magic" (Marc 1989: 118). Examples are *Bewitched* (1964) or *I Dream of Jeannie* (1965).

A step forward in the women movement was *The Mary Tyler Moore Show* in 1970, starring a divorced woman who tries to handle her career as well as her family. Then, as Bärmann (1993) claims, sitcoms seem to lose color because the topics are not that new and interesting anymore. *The Bill Cosby Show (1984)*, however, breathed life into the family sitcoms. So, the 1980s "sitcom attention shifted away from single people [...] and back toward the genre's traditional center: the family" (Marc 1989: 201). New shows like *Roseanne* (1988), featuring a strong woman as the main character, was appreciated in the USA as well as *Who is the boss?* (1984). Besides, ethnic sitcoms such as *The Bill Cosby Show* (1984) or *The Fresh Prince of Bel-Air* (1990) starring African Americans only, became very popular.

Nevertheless, the problems of single men and women are still an issue. Concentrating on the problems of single men and women have, is also quite popular in the 1980s and 1990s. In 1982, a sitcom about America's 'most famous bar' was broadcasted: *Cheers*. This series as well as *Friends* or *Golden Girls*, for instance, deal with relationships, jobs, and sexuality (Bärmann 1993: 17). The trend of leading a single-life and moving away from the traditional belief of the necessity of having a family comes up again.

2. Characteristics of sitcoms

The term *sitcom* derives from the word situation comedy. This popular format of entertainment is a weekly show that entails a regular cast of characters in a sequence of episodes which mainly take place in the same location. A sitcom is a make-believe for 24 minutes a week. Either series are taped in front of a studio audience or canned applause is taped in. Often sitcoms provide verbal plays, funny and unexpected situations, or problems which could happen to everyone and were rapidly resolved (http://www.answers.com/topic/situation-comedy).

Ross says that "[t]he humour in a sitcom comes from playing around with the comic possibilities of those particular character types interacting with each other in that situation, and may not involve lines or gags which are funny in isolation" (1998: 91).That means in contrast to telling a joke, a sitcom depends on the context in which humor is performed. This includes either utterances that proceed or follow the given utterance or the non-linguistic environment (Attardo 1994). Sitcom deal with areas the viewers can relate to and the atmosphere is intimate like being invited into the characters' home. Bärmann (1993) describes this as an escape from daily life for the audience.

In professional humor the communications as well as the characters are fictional. Most television programs use a standardized storytelling format having about three little stories which occur parallel. Mainly, there is one major story and two minor ones. This multilayered concept serves to make the sitcom more interesting and versatile. Each of the stories is based around a group of characters. Each of the themes has a three-act structure: the beginning, the middle, and the end (Bärmann, 1993: 3). The beginning introduces the thematic context, including a problem, a difficult decision, or any sort of action. The next section, the middle, contains an escalation, obstacles and sometimes various misunderstandings which is supposed to increase the tension of the show. In the end, everything is solved and everybody is more or less happy. Even though, surprise is an important and desirable element of comedy, quite often the end is fairly predictable[1]. Moreover, almost every sitcom starts with a short *teaser*. It is supposed to "quicken the appetite" of the audience by briefly showing the show's matters before the theme song is played. After the audience's attention is caught, the characters have about 24 minutes to resolve the problem and amuse the viewers. Subsequent to the final scene and the credits, comes a so called *tag*. It is about one minute long and can be seen as the final scene after the final scene (Mack 2002: 10). Holzer calls this the *signet* of the respective episode (1999: 22).

Furthermore, the characters of a sitcom are very important for good comedy. "The best situation comedy isn't about situations at all; it's about vulnerable people [...] comedy springs from character" (Armstrong quoted in Holzer 1999: 23). A sitcom depends on traditional stereotypes and repeated happenings or jokes like running gags because the audience needs to identify with the characters and the show in order to follow it continuously. Bärmann says that "the audience is expected to know who the characters are and why they are there. So the viewers have to be familiar with the series as a whole" (1993: 5). Knowing the background of the characters also supports that we identify with them, that we like them and suffer with them.

---

[1] Refer to Holzer (1999) for a detailed description of the technical and dramatic structure of the plot

Moreover, the studio audience and canned laughter, is typical for this new type of comedy. Some say that the desired positive effect of canned laughter is annoying for the audience in front of the TV. Due to my poll, only 4% of the German interrogates like canned laughter, whereas 29% of the Americans like it. This may also be because the Americans are rather used to it than Germans because in Germany sitcoms usually do not provide canned laughter at all.

Morreall claims that no one should spend too much time in front of the TV watching comedies because "there is always the danger of comedy having a morally damaging effect [...]" (1983: 5). Even though insulting other should not be funny, people enjoy well-expressed insults.

> The worst manifestation of our taste for this kind of laughter is probably the pitiful childish "situation comedies" that have glutted our television schedules for the past decades or so, many of which have almost no plot but consist of a group of family members or friends trading obvious and stupid insults (Morreall, 1983: 19).

To sum up, a sitcom is a daily or weekly show which is supposed to entertain the audience. Its little changes concerning location, characters, and actions are characteristic as well as the high amount of humor which arises in the situation.

Punch line, jab line

The positions of the lines in humorous texts can vary. A typical joke consists of a narrative and ends with a punch line. Longer texts, on the contrary, can have one or more jab lines. Sitcoms, for example, rather provide jab lines than punch lines. They do not disrupt the flow in which they occur, which is mainly a dialog between the characters and hardly ever one tells a joke. One story can consist of many smaller stories, each having its own jab or punch lines. Sitcoms consist of one main story including numerous small ones. Attardo illustrates how different types of texts can be illustrated (2001: 90):

-	non-humorous text (of any length)
→	end of narrative + material occurring after a punch line
J	jab line
P	punch line
[...]	beginning and end markers of a narrative
...	Any occurrence of – and J
⊦→	The beginning of the text

Table 1

A joke would be realized like that: [I→ - P→] and a story would be represented like this:

I→... [I → - P→] - [I → - J-J-P→] →

Attardo says that "[n]aturally, a punch line outside of an embedded narrative cannot subsist, which leaves us with three possibilities" (2001: 91). The punch line is either at the initial position, or at the final position, or at the pseudo-final position. Sitcoms, for instance start with a so-called *teaser* which is the opener of the show. Mainly, this is a joke or a gag, having no reference to the rest of the show. The closure of a sitcom is called *tag*. As well as the *teaser*, for the most part the *tag* has nothing to do with the rest of the show.

The pseudo-final position is almost identical to the final position. The only difference between them is "that the punch line occurs within level 0 narrative in a final punch line, whereas it occurs within level <0 narrative in a pseudofinal punch line" (Attardo 2001: 91).

2.1.   Strands and stacks

If punch or jab lines are thematically related, we speak of *strands*. Themes have to be repeated at least three times in order to be called *strands*. Many strands make up a *stack*. In sitcoms, this means that a strand makes up thematic related issues in one episode. Let us take the relationship between Ross and Rachel. A *stack* would be all strands referring to their relationship.

Repetition is an important tool for longer texts. Above all, sitcoms depend on reappearances. The audience knows what to expect and so they are set in the right mood to appreciate the show.

2.2.   Canned laughter

As mentioned above, the audience plays an important role and in a few sitcoms some guests are actually at the studio for the acoustic support. The desired effect of laughter can be achieved, if the audience is in a good mood. Greeting the audience, warming them up, and making them feel welcome are important, as Bärmann (1993) says. Sometimes, if the comments are not that funny, signs with the instruction to laugh are held up. To sum up, for a good show it is essential to "put the hearer(s) in the appropriate mood of expectation" (Raskin 1985: 12).

Marc adds that a sitcom "asks an audience to willingly suspend its disbelief, to forget that what it is seeing is artifice and contrivance" (1989: 11).

Additionally, Raskin states that one never likes laughs alone (1985: 17). People tend to laugh in company. "[T]here is a strong social aspect to the way people respond to humour" (Ross 1998: 1). When other people around you appreciate a joke, it is easier for you to do the same. However, the best comedy can be ruined by a bad audience. So, the reason why sitcoms provide canned laughter is that people in front of the TV have the feeling to laugh in company.

Viktoroff says:

> [...] One never laughs alone- laughter is always the laughter of a particular social
> group, and it is impossible to associate oneself with it if one does not share the
> group's norms, feelings and ideas – in short, if one is not part of it (quoted in
> Raskin 1985: 17).

Regarding sitcoms or other comedies, it may be easier and more pleasurable to laugh in company but it is not necessarily a condition for something to be humorous. It depends on whether you like the sort of humor or not because if you do, it is fairly common to laugh by oneself. Society, however, decides what is tolerated or forbidden (Raskin, 1985: 17).

Laughter of a studio audience transmits much more liveliness and vitality than canned laughter as Holzer (1999) states. Scenes seem to be more authentic with a real audience and true laughter than they are with imported canned laughter. The first show having a studio audience was *I love Lucy* in 1951. Nowadays, only a few sitcoms have a live audience. *Friends*, for example, performs in front of an audience and so maybe the laughter, we hear on TV seems more real than in other shows because about 80% of the imported laughter is real. The rest is added after the cutting. Other countries do not like to hear fake or even real laughter in the background. German sitcoms, for example, do not provide canned laughter at all (Holzer 1999: 17).

Humor and laughter are directly connected to one another since humor intends to provoke laughter. "More specifically, the presence of laughter is used in order to characterize an utterance or a text as humorous Laughter may come from the speaker while producing his/her own text or from the audience as a reaction to what is being said" (Archakis/Tsakona 2001: 44).

3. References (including additional literature)

Alexander, Richard J. 1997. Aspects of Verbal Humour in English. *Language in Performance 13.* Tübingen: Gunter Narr Verlag.

Antonopoulou, Eleni. 2004. Humor theory and translation research: Proper names in humorous discourse. *International Journal of Humor Research* 17. 219-255.

Archakis, Argiris and Villy Tsakona. 2005. Analyzing conversational data in GTVH terms: A new approach to the issue of identity construction via humor. *Humor* 18:1. 41- 68.

Attardo, Salvatore and Steven Brown, eds. 2000. *Understanding Language Structure, Interaction and Variation. An Introduction to Applied Linguistics and Sociolinguistics for Nonspecialists.* Michigan: The University of Michigan Press.

Attardo, Salvatore. 2001. *Humorous Texts: A Semantic and Pragmatic Analysis.* Humor Research 6. Berlin, New York: Mouton de Gruyter.

Bärmann, Christian. 1993. *Television Situation comedy in the U.S. and the U.K.* Unpublished MA thesis. English department. University of Hanover.

Beach, Christopher, ed. 2002. *Class, Language, and American Film Comedy.* Cambridge: University Press.

Belton, John, ed. 2005. *American Cinema / American Culture.* Second edition. New York: The McGraw-Hill Companies.

Berelson, Bernard. 1952. *Content Analysis in Communication Research.* New York: Hafner Publishing Company.

Borchers, Hans, Gabriele Kreutzner und Eva-Maria Warth. 1994. *Never-ending Stories: American Soap Operas and the Cultural Production of Meaning.* Trier: Wissenschaftlicher Verlag.

Bremmer, Jan and Herman Roodenburg, eds. 1999. *Kulturgeschichte des Humors. Von der Antike bis heute.* Darmstadt: Primus Verlag. (9-17)

Chapman, Anthony J. and Hugh C. Foot, eds. 1976. *Humour and Laughter.* London etc.: John Wiley & Sons.

Coleman, Earle J. 1985. The Funnies, the Movies and Aesthetics. *Journal of Popular Culture* 18:4. 89-100.

Critchley, Simon. 2002. *On Humour. Thinking in Action.* London, New York: Routledge.

Davies, Christie, ed. 1990. *Ethnic Humor Around the World. A Comparative Analysis.* Bloomington, Indiana: Indiana University Press.

Davies, Christie. 1998. Jokes and their Relation to Society. *Humor Research 4.* Berlin, New York: Mouton de Gruyter.

Freud, Sigmund. 1905. *Jokes and their relation to the unconscious.* Translated by James Stachley. Standard Edition Vol. 8. London: Hogarth Press (1957).

Goldstein, Laurence. 1990. The linguistic interest of verbal humor. *International Journal of Humor Research* 3. 37-52.

Gruner, Charles R. 1976. Wit and Humour in Mass Communication. In: Chapman, Antony J. and Hugh C. Foot, eds. 1976. *Humour and Laughter.* London etc.: John Wiley & Son. 287-312.

Günther, Ulrike. 2002. What's in a laugh. Humour, jokes and laughter in the conversational corpus of the BNC. Inaugural Dissertation, Freiburg.

Hausendorf, Heiko. 2000. *Zugehörigkeit durch Sprache. Eine linguistische Studie am Beispiel der deutschen Wiedervereinigung.* Reihe Germanistische Linguistik. Tübingen: Nax Niemeyer Verlag.

Holzer, Daniela. 1999. *Die deutsche Sitcom. Format-Konzeption-Drehbuch-Umsetzung.* Bergisch Gladbach: Bastei-Verlag Gustav H. Lübbe GmbH & Co.

Keller, Harald. 1999 *Kultserien und ihre Stars. Nebst einer "Vorbemerkung eines Serienhelden" von Harry Rowohlt*. Reinbek bei Hamburg: Rowohlt   Taschenbuch Verlag GmbH.

Kotthoff, Helga, ed. 1996. *Scherzkommunikation. Beiträge aus der empirischen Gesprächsforschung*. Opladen: Westdeutscher Verlag.

Kotthoff, Helga. 1998. *Spaß Verstehen. Zur Pragmatik von konversationellem Humor*. Reihe Germanistische Linguistik 196. Tübingen: Max Niemeyer Verlag GmbH & Co. KG.

La Fave, Lawrence et al. Superiority, Enhanced Self-Esteem, and Perceived Incongruity Humour Theory. In: Chapman, Antony J. and Hugh C. Foot, eds. 1976. *Humour and Laughter*. London etc.: John Wiley & Son. 63-92.

Le Goff, Jacques. 1999. Lachen im Mittelalter. In: Bremmer, Jan and Herman   Roodenburg, eds. *Kulturgeschichte des Humors. Von der Antike bis heute.*   Darmstadt: Primus Verlag. 43-56.

Lempp, Reinhart. 1992. Das Lachen des Kindes. Das Lachen in der psychischen Entwicklung. In: Vogel, Thomas, ed. *Vom Lachen: einem Phänomen auf der   Spur*. Tübingen: Attempto Verlag. 79-92.

McGhee, Paul E. 1979. *Humor. Its Origin and Development*. San Francisco: W.H. Freeman and Company.

Marc, David. 1989. *Comic Visions. Television Comedy and American Culture*. London, Worcester: Billing & Sons.

Marshall, Jill and Angela Werndly. 2002. *The Language of Television*. Intertext. London: Routledge.

Mintz, Lawrence E. 1999. American humor as unifying and divisive. *International Journal of Humor Research* 12. 237-252.

Morreall, John. 1983. *Taking Laughter Seriously*. Albany: State University of New   York Press.

Morreall, John. 1989. Enjoying incongruity. *International Journal of Humor Research* 2. 1-18.

Nerhardt, Göran. 1976. Incongruity and Funniness: Towards a New Descriptive Model. In: Chapman, Antony J. and Hugh C. Foot, eds. 1976. *Humour and Laughter*.   London etc.: John Wiley & Son. 55-62.

Oring, Elliott. 1992. *Jokes and Their Relations*. Kentucky: The University Press of Kentucky.

Oxford. Advanced Learner's Dictionary. 2000. 6th edition. Oxford: University Press

Paton, George E.C. 1988. The Comedian as Portrayer of Social Morality. In: Powell,   Chris and George E. Paton, eds. *Humour in Society. Resistance and Control*.   New   York: St. Martin's Press. 206-233.

Pollio, Howard R. and John W. Edgerly. 1976. Comedians and Comic Style. In: Chapman, Antony J. and Hugh C. Foot, eds. 1976. *Humour and Laughter*.   London etc.: John Wiley & Son. 215-244.

Popcorn, Faith. 1996. *"Clicking". Der neue Popcorn Report. Trends für unsere Zukunft. Von Clanning bis zu Cyberpools. Neue Ideen für das Jahr 2000*. München: Wilhelm Heyne Verlag.

Powell, Chris. 1988. A Phenomenological Analysis of Humour in Society. In: Powell,   Chris and George E. Paton, eds. *Humour in Society. Resistance and Control*.   New   York: St. Martin's Press. 86-105.

Raskin, Victor. 1985. *Semantic Mechanisms of Humor*. Synthese Language Library 24. Dordrecht etc.: D. Reidel Publishing Company.

Richard, Alexander J. 1997. *Aspects of Verbal Humour in English*. Language in Performance. Tübingen: Gunter Narr Verlag.

Ritchie, Graeme. 2004. *The Linguistic Analysis of Jokes*. London, New York: Routledge.

Ross, Alison. 1998. *The Language of Humour.* Intertext. London, New York: Routledge.

Rothbart, Mary R. 1976. Incongruity, Problem-Solving and Laughter. In: Chapman, Antony J. and Hugh C. Foot, eds. 1976. *Humour and Laughter.* London etc.:   John Wiley & Son. 37-54.

Schneider, Irmela, ed. 1995. *Serien-Welten. Strukturen US-Amerikanischer Serien aus   vier Jahrzehnten.* Opladen: Westdeutscher Verlag GmbH.

Schutz, Charles E. 1989. The sociability of ethnic jokes. *International Journal of Humor Research* 2. 165-177.

Shultz, Thomas R. 1976. A Cognitive-Developmental Analysis of Humour. In: Chapman, Antony J. and Hugh C. Foot, eds. *Humour and Laughter*: London etc.: John Wiley & Sons. 11-36.

Simpson, Paul. 2003. *On the discourse of satire.* Philadelphia and Amsterdam: John Benjamins.

Taylor, Paul. 1988. Scriptwriters and Producers: A Dimension of Control in Television Situation Comedies. In: Powell, Chris and George E. Paton, eds. *Humour in Society. Resistance and Control.* New York: St. Martin's Press. 179-205.

Trudgill, Peter. 1983. *Sociolinguistics: An introduction to language and society.* Harmondsworth: Penguin Books.

Trudgill, Peter. 1974. *Sociolinguistics. An introduction.* Harmondsworth: Penguin Books.

Tueth, Michael V. 2005. *Laughter in the Living Room.* New York etc.: Peter Lang.

Van Giffen, Katherine and Kathleen M. Maher. 1995. Memorable humorous incidents: gender, themes and setting effects. *International Journal of Humor Research* 8. 39-50.

Vogel, Thomas, ed. 1992. *Vom Lachen: einem Phänomen auf der Spur.* Tübingen: Attempto Verlag.

Weber, Robert Philip. 1990. *Basic Content Analysis*, 2nd ed. Newbury Park: Sage publications.

Weiderer, Monika. 1993. *Das Frauen- und Männerbild im Deutschen Fernsehen. Eine inhaltsanalytische Untersuchung der Programme ARD, ZDF und RTL plus.* Regensburg: S. Roderer Verlag.

Wickeberg, Daniel. 1998. *The Senses of Humor. Self and Laughter in Modern America.* Ithaca and London: Cornell University Press.

Wild, David. 2004. *Friends …'till the end. The One With All Ten Years.* Warner Bros. Entertainment Inc. London: Headline book publishing.

Internet sources/ URLs:

- Chi square. URL: http://schnoodles.com/cgi-bin/web_chi_form.cgi. Accessed February 7th, 2007.
- Content Analysis. URL: http://writing.colostate.edu/guides/research/content/pop2a.cfm. Accessed January 13th, 2007.
- Encyclopaedia. URL: http://open-encyclopedia.com. Accessed December 14th, 2006.
- Friends. URL: http://www.geocities.com/friends_greatestsitcom/poll.htm. Accessed February 12th, 2007.
- Friends. URL: http://www.hollywoodjesus.com/friends.htm. Accessed February 5th, 2007.
- Friends. URL: http://www.tv.com. Accessed February 21st, 2007.
- Humor. URL: http://www.iep.utm.edu/h/humor.htm. Accessed December 1st, 2006.
- Humor. URL: http://wwwhome.cs.utwente.nl/~anijholt/artikelen/ctit24_2002.pdf. Accessed January 22nd, 2007.
- Transcripts. URL: http://www.friendstranscripts.tk. Accessed February 26th, 2007.
- Sitcom. URL: http://www.periwork.com/peri_db/civi_db/2002_May_2_18_34_23/index2.html. Accessed February 5th, 2007.
- Sitcom. URL: http://www.answers.com/topic/situation-comedy. Accessed January 12th, 2007.
- Wissen. URL: http://www.wissen.de. Accessed December 10th, 2006

For further information about this subject see „The American way of comedy. A comprehensive analysis of humor on the basis of the US sitcom ‚Friends'" by Irina Wamsler.

ISBN: 978-3-638-81741-7

http://www.grin.com/en/e-book/78804/